Duncan McNaughton

Valparaíso

"Vale of Paradise," perhaps. Like New Orleans, an old port city where the barrier, or veil, between the living and the dead, is thinner than usual. From the wharves at its wide bay, Valparaíso rises like an open fan up steep hills which ascend directly from the Pacific...effect of an immense amphitheatre. Standing on rooftops high enough on those hills, one looks east over the coast range, across all of slender Chile, to the Andes sharp and snowy in a clear blue sky. All the way to Aconcagua, highest of all, away in Argentina. In reality, like they say, a tough city, though not mean, and extremely beautiful, full of brilliant corners and the colors of bright paint.

Listening Chamber
Berkeley
1995

For having first printed versions of many of these poems, *Thanks* to Franco Beltrametti (*Bollettario*), Franco Beltrametti & Dario Villa (*codice biancaneve*), Philippe Castellin & Jean Torregrosa (*DOC(K)S*), Lee Chapman (*First Intensity*), Andrei Codrescu (*Exquisite Corpse*), Pierre Coupey (*Capilano Review*), Stephen Ellis (*:that:* and *OASII*), Stefan Hyner (*Gate*), Jay Knoepfl & Jesse Taylor-York (*Prosodia*), Nathaniel Mackey (*Hambone*), Jean Monod (*AIOU*), Charlie Ross (*Smithereens*), Pat Smith & Drew Gardner (*Notus*), and to the soul of Leland Hickman (*Temblor*).

The author here records his gratitude to Etel Adnan for her illuminated calligraphic version of a portion of *Black Spoon*; to Kora McNaughton for her photographs of Valparaíso; to Marianne Kolb for her aquatint; to the Arts Council of Marin County, California; and to Tina Rotenberg and Steve Dickison.

Typesetting and design by Steve Dickison.
Printed on acid-free paper

Valparaíso is published as Listening Chamber Poetry Series No. 2 in 1995
by:
LISTENING CHAMBER
1605 Berkeley Way
Berkeley, California 94703

VALPARAÍSO

TABLE OF CONTENTS

to

KID

"life" begins to "end" "about" [what] "form"

Clear Spot

When the morning calls in, that golden bird
when it's over, that golden metaphysical bird
when the meaning calls, I am in

There were no gold birds in the meaning
other than golden, the metaphysical birds

"Those little golden birdies, look at them"

---

to Lee Hickman 23 June 89

To Sarah Menefee

Some clumsy way to say that the victory
is a friend, that deliverance and betrayal
are the same thing, that age and death
will have their volition but neither is
a fountainhead of understanding, that
one's freedom is one's love and one's love
is one's undoing, it's all in the dictionary —
who can vindicate himself?

A system of weights and graces rising on the wing
as if

"Cuántos me faltan, sombras del canto, compañeros..."

Are you all really just dead?
Or are you there,
in that dazzling sunlight
y esas sombras griegas,
playing cards again
at those old wooden tables,
smoking strong tobacco,
some taverna
on some island
where I've never been?

Today the weather here
is perfect also,
except that I miss you.
       Come nearer,
my friends,
I need a hand.
My life
and my poems,
they're perfect too,
right?
      Your songs sound sweet today
in the music of thoughts
like this one.
Incomparable men
I knew face to face.
The day doesn't pass
but that I reach
for your hands.

We needed someone to be, they
said, so
we became you.

What about me?

You are not you
nor are you us.

Music inside the body,
               music outside the body, often they pass
down a lane which isn't anywhere,
so often we fail to notice
when the songs
change place.

I expect the music never stops
         though we do.

What had been the question
             concerning what we must live in
                 order to do here?

Deep music,
             slow music, seems
not to progress
                   but to measure
       a form of containment.

Breathing is an exchange of air.
        Like everything else we are breathing.

Purple Gate

Coming back
in
Mesa Road
middle morning
standing
at the roadside
eyes brilliant
face handsome
shoulders broad
chest strong
beautifully
shaped
antlers
at the peak
of his youth
moved
like a prince
in the forest
might —
face to face
before we met.

When he paced away
barely touching
the ground there was
no sound
anywhere
in the world —
eucalyptus trees
sun light
pouring through.

Ode to the smell of firewood

Late, with the stars
wide open in the cold,
I opened the door.

                              Ocean

galloping
in the night.

Almost like a hand
of the darkened house
the intense aroma
of the woodpile
gripped me.

I could practically see the smell
as
if the tree
was still alive.
As if still throbbing.

Visible
as an overcoat.

Visible
as the aroma of a broken branch.

I walked
back into
the house
surrounded

by that balsamic
darkness.
Outside
the bright points
of the sky were sparkling
like magnetic stones,
and the smell of the firewood
held on to me, held on
to my heart
like someone's fingers
like jasmine
like some memories do.

It wasn't the sharp smell
of pine,
no,
it wasn't
the smell like when you rupture the skin
of the eucalyptus,
it wasn't
the green perfumes
of the vine
either,
but instead
something more secret,
because that fragrance
existed only
once,
and, of all the places I've seen in the world, there
in my own
house, at night, together with a wintry ocean,

it was waiting for me,
the smell
of the most profound rose,
the heart cut out of the earth:
something
came over me like a wave
disconnected
from time
and I got lost
in who I am,
just then,
when I opened the door
to night.

Oda al olor de la leña, Pablo Neruda

Noctiluca

After
dark a
lifetime
still
rendering
itself

calmed
for
a few minutes
by sirens
who make no sound
nor need they.

A glass of clear water, a tumbler on the grass mat, haze

There, off to the right, a blue pond
boys come to row there

light, season, the orders of their hour

to places they will never be able to forget
the mud the tufted footpads at the edge

Then a wan winter sky stone benches stone balustrades they haven't
invented it but they know what to do with it
they are after all

                    they can salvage now they are
                        to lose possession of it

---

to Daniel

A small dinette in the country

Even the desperately ill, the bone-weary
the jailed, even the innocent
children, cows in the field, even the lambs
that lie away on rocky hillsides
wreathed in fog, for that matter the fog itself
and the cars parked under dim
fog-wreathed street lamps,
even the very drowsy shrouded street lamps too:
how anyone can sleep tonight
on this continent
is beyond me.

How invisibly crowded around midnight
the foggy darkness with its
aura of voices
aghast
at the anniversary:
another year of having done all in our power
to keep still
our hearts lest their furious
pain explode like lava upon the mind, that
ghost,
the I-deny-I-am-the-witness.

America is the modern world,
it has been the modern world for 500 years,
the stairway to heaven, ladder to the stars
l'ascenseur pour l'échafaud.

Let them speak, the everlasting dead

we were born into
to remember
the coming
into
matter of the earth
and its end. Men
and women, our hands
and time
fallen
falling apart.

In church the winds of outer space
moaned so sadly, open or
shut I never cared for the casket
or its wintry flowers, I wanted planets
starry destinations which could never end
I was a child then, sounds meant
the world to me,
rubbery
automobile tires rumbling
across the wood planks of a railroad bridge,
clock chimes from a distant room.

And what about the voices the night
air filled with
over the rooftops,
voices
which made the trees so still?
No one mentioned those voices,
those so sweet dark voices deep
as the sky,
no one talks about them now
either. I wonder why.

Ache,
one never shakes it,
for home, so far away
no matter where you are,
that's where they call from.

The real sound of our
ordinary world,
too much
with us, too obvious, too
overwhelmingly
inside us,
is the call or
strangely chiming song
identical with the air,
with any sound one ever hears,
yet still
we nearly never pay attention,
so much inside us
we scarcely know we hear it:
how in the world
can that be?

Is it the sound of the voices of family love?
Is the profound
tenderness of meek affections for linked companions stored away
in the sadness of knowledge?
Is the first knowledge of farewell?
Is the final knowledge
a vision
which that farewell

releases us
into, we who
never could
say farewell,
we who deformed
our hearts
to resist
the scheme
which commanded us
to forget
the legendary
voices
who taught us
to love
the most ancient
images
of knowing
who we are
again
on earth?

———————

to Io

The Year of the Woman

But Emily
was a man,
Alice —

all
men
were.

Lucky At Cards

The movie played a comedy about the wrong number
of lovers played by stars given words to say
the way a perfect stranger is taken over by the same one
who writes movie talk and gives motion to the heavens
and becomes one of those beings so new to life on earth
so perfect so strange so puzzled by the monetary system

What do you mean by asking "What does it want to say?"
it wasn't trying to convince anyone it was a movie
it's not the fault of words that they don't know anything

After midnight like silk flowers in dim hours
bright notes trumpet

At An Advanced Hour Del Siglo

If history has been a man or
for that matter a divinity, un viejo
mulish, shambling through his atmosphere
petering out long after midnight
his rooms redolent of his farts
another vulgar exhaustion, *Goddamit*
how long have all the fucking light bulbs been blown
after so many, still plotting
one last epochal humiliation
one last mess on the floor, one last
catastrophically mean expression of bad taste
Let them clean up their own fucking fates
when he is dead who will have the balls to tell him
he is dead, we are all out of eggs.

Therefore the night that
windy desolation of outer darkness:
somewhere a cat of all creatures mocks the mind in heat.

If nature has been a woman
or a goddess for that matter, una vieja
who preys on her children
on her children's children
because they are children;
the two of them those two old cretins
it's not true they disagree

history and genetics don't disagree.

Por eso, what's an old poet to do
por supuesto, to bathe
             each day in anise-scented waters
one or two answers to anyone who asks
             if not honest, then harmonious
a look in the mailbox, just in case:

nothing, in other words, which might compromise
the absence, la ausencia
de la luz.

Strophe

"You are...?" I asked. "Trace,"
he replied, "keener than most persons."
Hurriedly I explained my mission as the scent
of skunk poured through the unshuttered
fenestration like gas must, into
a prison death chamber, mist
bearing its stench of unlucky choice

bitter shake
rolling
between my fingers

every degradation of the Nineties was stinking
up the dump off a back alley I'd rented stoutly
resolved to leave no joker face down while she
dogged me around and then to cut loose for
old blue skies. "Brisk eyes," he observed in the snap

of her held in his hand, "an unexamined wife,
a real gravel pit Annie. I'll start right away."
The hour was a flower when the odor of disorder
everted and two guys turned
into two men of the cloth
plotting the pillars where the temple once stood.

---

to Doc Meltzer

Red lightning, red feathers

So she had stopped at the roadside where the two
girls had their table and bought the earrings
from them which they had made, high coral pink
held in silver, she was wearing them and
the instant he noticed he elected to lie
as if the way the talk was going needed it,
the lie was compositional, harmed no one and
set loose meanings which the universe
hadn't planned on.

Oh, I thought you were telling the truth,
she said, and he had, you see,
right through his teeth, no explaining it
like Africa, all those reds everywhere all the time:
white people don't belong here, she said.

Hey, 'Abbas! he cried. How much longer do I have
to live? From Spain to the Cape of Tormentoso,
she said, is a huge organ rather like a heart but
swollen by its brain like the explanation
for why you need to lie to me. 'Abbas shrugged
and walked back to the counter wondering why
it had been called darkest by outsiders:
her brother had given her a new car which she had driven
around the interior, it stood on the road outside, blue.

———————————

to Diana

Home

Midpath overturned shopping cart's
seat for a man missing an eye, left:
drinks from a tequila pint, carton
orange juice back. Sunrise

in the northern desplobado, dawn
where Branciforte Creek's San Quentinish
flood containment trough curves from Water
to Ocean. I would join you

absolutely, I reply, but my liver, lately,
has seen daylight. Oh, man,
that's a drag. I'll say a prayer
for you, man, God bless you. Barbed

metal fences, late Californian motel
backyards, opaque sliding windows, shower sounds,
toilet gurgle: the creek behind Bariteau's
Linen Service and the really used car lot.

Vice-regal creek, cement zoo.
Two hundred years ago on the bluff above us
el proiecto de una nueva población
where this morning's supermarket furniture

makes do for my sympathetic acquaintance's
a.m. eye opener, as the stream below's
meagre trickle through prison pavement's
home to a family of bathing ducks.

Poem

Usefulness
drains out eagerly!
rainwater through a riddle

eager branches off a plum tree
arranged in a spray, slender
black branches, white flowers
white petals
                        falling to the floor

like that famous photograph from Spain
the young fighter at the instant he died
arching backward falling forward arms flung upward
to the sun
their eagerness slain at the instant they were cut

think of them as divinely transformed
into objects of beauty
their lives

on the radio I heard a Russian woman
say the words petit bourgeois
exactly the right way

What part of the chicken is this?

Somewhere, though not far,
south of Idleton,
alongside a rutted road

which the hens cross all day long,
lies the town of Simpleton:
I live there now,

and in the hour before the lamp's
extinguished, under a feathery quilt
I read from the pages of Henri Beyle,
warmed by the flanks de ma poule.

"How are we to be amused by ordinary object art?"
I asked Igor Hallinan. "Robinson, that's Nigel
Robinson," he said. We had left the lecture early
enough to spot the 1940s, Robinson nudged me,
ducking into a beanery behind the hotel, chinoise,
and hurried to follow Laura through its rear door
which opened into a room where women sat
　　　　along the walls
braced by orange straps across their foreheads,
mouths open to receive rubbery shafts with heads
on them like nothing so much as parts of the body
men love most. The switch was thrown convulsing
them with shocks, followed by a temporary euphoria.
A shimmering mist showered the room, I felt it
enter my pores. "They are all wives,"
Nigel explained, "whose husbands represent stability."

¿Ars breva etiam más breva vita, no?

One so seldom hears the expression "Eastern
    Hemisphere" any more
rising as it once did toward the midnight of clouds
very like the noise of an evening of good loving
    and many beers of dancing hard
with one's belle nanchon

brains of America, all you know.

Not one teardrop fallen
      but that we were

   ...just a thought.

Wee children dropping through the sky
bent
  toward the bosom of the bear.

Through one temple out the other

Years playing trombone in a Christian orchestra
one night the mood left me, what can I tell you

the piano player took my hand in hers
and put both between her legs, so I split

them while I could still see in
black and white.

_____

to Dorothy Lazard

Even, 4th of July This Year

Vous tous, from Cape Breton to Chiloe
all you americas, you've led the way

to the most puzzling
contradiction

your secularity
competes
against the secularity
of God

as for the me of my name,
what other choice do I have
than to oppose both of you?

Product

I was good at what I done and I done it
and whenever I walk through

                               an empty room I swerve, twice
               to avoid the memories
what I have wanted out of all this was a dame
             if there's a dame
                    you don't care about nothing
except her

He could have been absolutely anyone
The Sphinx some Coptic letters some Arabic
             They are so smart these guys
                 Mire,   sus cuerpos luminosos...

Why waste time
           I couldn't do nothing with her
        so I turned her over

                 to some Sappho on a Harley

"With the inconceivable patience of disillusionment"

At four in the morning almost
waked by the imperial hiss of spigots
spitting reclaimed water on parched grass
by the path underneath the elevated train track
too much red wine to stay asleep
its retributive dream
      too near the surface of the membrane

too much like the men Bolívar represents
in the story by García Márquez
disordered saints who imagine they love women
who in turn assassinate them with day-long nights

Enough to have been slugged like a heavy bag
for 175 years por el puño del norte
having to explain himself over and over again
to women who treat him like a child
or like a divinity, whichever they think is worse

Such a man walks like an insomniac
      through the hegemony
his thoughts in almost exact agreement
with those of the contrary gender:
what other use is there to a man
than to get hard and be milked?

After four-thirty a timer somewhere inside
a grey metal box shuts down the spray

Such a man takes pleasure in the silence
near dawn
because he belongs to it
he hopes that after the end the same silence
may take him, in her arms
the way a girl does,
the one who hasn't ever stood before a mirror.

The cost of living has gone way down
th'expense of shame in a waist —
no, in a waste of shame —
th'expense of spirit in a waist of shame
has gone down too.

What's that going up?
rising to my Mistress Gam?

ham & garter
hand in glove,

winter snow
through frosty glass.

Old northern aire:

                         bathing promise,

never mourn.

               Cold moon.

Since When

You know you're fifty
don't bother looking for your heart

it's perdido

⋆

late at night the traffic's light
radio stations come so clear
            when you reach September
driving alone
tires swishing wet leaves
            or dreams
that you're here, close to me

⋆

when the weather was this cool she wore
a fox stole with its I'm not
the kind of a girl
            for a boy like you
little blue
glass eyes

⋆

cuándo está lluviando allí
en los barrios
de Boston
        the streets are black and slick
                this time of year

all the lights and trees that gleam of
all the rainy pleasures late at night
traffic's light
fingers hardly touch the wheel

*

saw it all from a window, still do:
holiday tables, under the trees...

it isn't *even* April
no hay castañas por aquí

*

isn't there something else about her
that she mustn't end

there'll be others who can't help being young
inside lives that get old and wry, not even
asking why

they're perdido too

★

not like her though
                    since when

"I love *you*"

_____

Valentine's 1992

At Once A Few Cities

Miles of air, miles of sea, what else made
    the world
compact, than an orchestra
in the movies, on the radio years ago
the elevated train drowned out.
Away in Argentina? Why, just over the Andes,
    same way the weather goes.

Didn't you ever fly
     above the Carib sea,
watching the sun
     rise over Cuba?

    How I touched on Panamá
is explained, more or less, by the days I used to know:
those clear triangular notes
they're all in the blue
what causes the bay to be so green
the lake in the park too,
     it seemed so much
to hope for,
Gorkys to look at,
but it wasn't. The old de Koonings
made Dutch bulbs flash
and on the wall opposed a wall of Klines.
By the time I'd finished hanging out the wash
the first of it was dry
about this time of year.

---

to Jennifer Griffith

Poem

Like if I was a pretty white blackberry blossom
alone some night by a dusty road
tossing in the savage wind
unbeknown to God
I'd consider it good luck
that a handsome man passed by
and shined his lantern on my face
long enough to fall in love
                                        Why hesitate?
Chances like that are rare
though of course it's what the two of us
are living for.

Sugarcane

She was a girl I knew when we were kids
we got wet at the same time
we could hardly help it
indoors or outside
everything was dripping
rags hanging from the window sills were soaked
Holding hands felt like moist
moon light on the banana leaves
Flags limp, stumps for easy chairs, lamp posts
gilded by aureoles of gold bugs
enhanced the sensation
perspiration on her upper lip
urgent pores.

———————————————

homenajito a Luis Cernuda

Buffets of wind rock the pickup truck, sea lions
split rail fence, silver greens flattened by the wind
looking northeast to where the houses simply and neatly
designed stand apart among rocks no trees mute windows
girls on the road after school dressed like when my mother
was a kid only with shoes
coffee from a white plastic cup, very good coffee
There never was a more beautiful spring time
not a poor man at all, that's just it, pale cliffs
I was walking at the shore of the new world
the sound of my heart which I can't forget forever
resounds, fishing boats down below moored trembling
in a stiff chop, serene moon, kinesis of the bay
the sound of it opens the window of a room

---

to Ken Irby

Dreams of Trains

The trains were dreaming
in the station, defenseless,
without locomotives, asleep.

I entered one, staggering, at dawn:
I'd gone there looking for secrets,
things left behind in the coaches,
in the dead odor of the journey.
Between the bodies which had departed
I took a seat, alone, on the unmoving train.

The air was compact, a block
of lapsed conversations, fugitive disappointments,
souls left behind on the trains
like keys without locks
dropped under the seats.

Passengers from the South, women burdened
with bouquets and poultry,
maybe they'd been murdered,
maybe they'd come back here and wept,
maybe they had exhausted the coaches
with the fire of their carnations:
maybe I'm travelling, I am among them,
maybe the steam of the journeys,
the wet rails, maybe
it's all alive in the unmoving train
and I a sleepy passenger
miserably awakened.

I was sitting there and the train
was running inside my body,
annihilating my frontiers:
all at once it was the train of my infancy,
smoky mist at daybreak,
summer's joy, bitter summer.
There were other trains speeding by,
carriages so full of grief
they groaned as if loaded with asphalt:
and thus the unmoving train raced on
in the morning which grew
so sadly over my bones.

I was alone on that solitary train,
yet not only I was alone,
but like a congregation of fates, so many solitudes
had crowded together there,
hoping to travel far away
like the poor who wait on station platforms.
And I in the train like a dead wraith
among so many unlucky creatures, ungraspable,
bent over by so many deaths,
I felt lost on a journey
in which nothing was moving
except my tired heart.

Sueños de Trenes, Pablo Neruda

Valparaíso

"She contains all, nothing is lacking"

Whitman sojourned in New Orleans long enough
to notice that prostitutes would be whores
if one allowed oneself to describe women
with no enormities of any sort
a hard caste to comprehend.

One winter Sunday morning on an empty street
in Temuco I sat alone in a truck, smoking cigarettes
and watching for the continents to take up their
fountain pens so that a huge white egg
balanced on the back of an old brown horse
would appear or in the same sense
a poet with very big balls
se llama Pablo Huevón

———————

to Kora

Blood Count

3:31 a.m. Friday April 26 This Year

I call upon the tutors
I call upon the real magic realism of Walt Whitman
            upon the twenty love poems of Pablo Neruda
            upon the John Thomas of David Lawrence
I call upon the souls of every unjust death
                of every creature entity and idea since time began
I call upon the souls of every innocently suffering living being
                thing and desire in every universe of space-time
I am not making a prayer I am publishing the call

I call upon the Angel Intellect of humanity
        I call upon the Exile within Whom creation
                    dreams its own end
I call upon the double suicides of Chikamatsu
I call upon al-Shaikh al-Akbar upon every tear he wept
                upon Rumi and Shams
                        I call upon the ghost of Billy Strayhorn
I call upon the wrath of Khiḍr
        upon the King of the Kingdom of Jesus Christ
I call upon Shiva the Flame rising from the couch of fucking
        upon all the ponies of China grazing on meadow flowers
I call upon the summation of Malcolm X
            upon Sappho her sacraments of marriage
                upon the foreign impurity of Robert Duncan
                    forgiven by Arthur Rimbaud

I call upon the buttocks of Neal Cassady
                    why not?
I call upon the spiral curves of John Milton's hair
            upon Thoth that monkey masturbating his knob

I call upon the night of sleep of my mother
I call upon my father dreaming their last kiss

I call upon the wind in my window blinds
            blown from every shore on earth
                    to my room this dark morning

Now that it's two minutes too late
            to defend anything
                        I call upon Dionysos
                            to laugh
                                through his hollow mask

I call upon the Emptiness of all powers
Nothing can defend us therefore
            I call upon it

O, ancestor Absence I call upon You
        upon the blink of Your Eye
            upon the dew on Your Cheek

        disarm the sellers and buyers of our equity
            shake them out
        humble them to clean the mess they have made
            of the purpose of being people

To dispel their every bungled chemistry
I call upon the velocity
                    of the perfume
                              of the nakedness
                of my wife after four a.m.
            waked in sleepy affection
                              to surround the world

I call upon Peace of Mind.

So, nun du mich kennst

When your back is turned the years run away —
run away where?
I know:
              they race after one another like happy children
to a happy place where all their friends await them,
heaven on earth,
                    or at least where the two realms meet:
a heart, full of all the things that ever happened.
How did you alone make every one of them possible?

Now they're waiting there for you
to join them like the years do
when finally you're cut loose too.

Of course, what happens after that, can anybody know?
It seems that faraway place which is also so very near
everts itself and disappears,
though it leaves behind a sort of residue or dust to show
those who cared for you what's inside them every day.

The Death of Lee Hickman

Who could describe the tattoos on her torso?
>The gypsy queen my ass she was Irish.

Well whoever she was she wasn't with me.
Huge nipples though and a saucy mouth probably Polish.

She could have been French. "If you look at my legs
another minute I'm going to humiliate you."

"I'm not looking at your legs I'm looking between them."
She agreed to tell me all I asked if I proved to her
>I spoke more Zingarrijib than she.

I had lied to her her legs were paramount
>on them she ran through the darkness of night
fleeing those little friends of the trees the squirrels
I had put there as my mind was the nocturne itself.

For hours we contested her tongue
>until the word for gun
revealed to me she'd come from Hungary.
"That's my red car over there bathed in silver moonlight."

Her blue eyes brightened beneath her bonnet:
"You are no gentleman you are a devil."

---

to Charles McCauley

Avenue Foch

Aversion to monument, its annual weight

neige   nuage

      Order me a double

who dresses well and has some money in his wallet
some form of golem equipped with all my sensations
Let him handle the passage of time
                the numbly juxtaposed
words
      Let him be the equivalent
              Let him market the mask

à Jean Monod

To Davis Rogan

From where I now
sit
writing measures

distance in the
dust
ascends a sun

lit air. Ere that
dust
descends there'll be

no echo, no
rhyme,
nor wonder how:

what it is we
are
made for is what

a parade's for.

BLACK SPOON

Estamos en Cuculandia
and how humiliating to be conscious of it
Lucho Argaín / Anton Chekhov

Say what   be more than the   sadly defeating

               wise-ass   smartness

                                              of the age

say what faith   what form

                 of

work   by

          which a man

                        can shake off

humiliation.

         In the exchange of one's life

for one's art   form

           communicates   the body

                  in the dark:

un feuillet   a leaf   a page

some   thing like a

                                                          leap of

            faith

                        undefaced.

                                    Whose mind

deregulated   mine

            in the northern   cone

                              who

disappeared me   dans le royaume

                                                          des ténèbres

                  mithl

Iskandar   ma'

            Khiḍr?

                                          I   woke up

            asking,   Where are the lilacs?

                                              And where the

open   metaphysics   of the

                                                          poppies?

Where's the rain

that was unceasingly

beating down

its words

filling them with pinholes

and birds? La

metafísica cubierta de

amapolas

llegaba a la cuchara negra:

en forma

de Ellington opium Ivie

and you.

I'll explain.

I was alive

in a suburb

of San Francisco, con campanas, con

relojes,

con

árboles. Desde allí

se veían   los rostros

          amargos   de las

                    américas,

                    like   an ocean

of leathery   assholes.

                    My house   was called the house

                              of

flowers   because from every   doorway, every open

                              window

                                        burst out

          geraniums,

                    a beautiful house

                                        with dogs

and kids.   Pablo,   you

                    remember.

                                        Do you

remember,   Robert?

                                        Federico, do you

          remember

from   under the   earth,

        can you   remember

            my   house   of

                              children, my   house

                              of   dogs

where the light   of May

            drowned   las amapolas

            en tu boca?

                                    Remember,

Simone, la lumière   humide

                              de la mangue?

        Etel,

                    te souviens-tu

        les cerises   douce-amères?

                                    Blood's river,

Nahr Ibrahim,   some Adonis

        of inexplicable   irony gushing

                    through   Lebanon

            to the sea.

54

What

could I fail   to observe

                from my house?   How can I   explain?

                        The lilacs

        never had   disappeared.

                                                        My room

when I awoke

                        suffocated me

        with its rank   stench   of lilacs

                                        rooted

in the buried   faces   and humid

                memories   of

                mildewed gods.

...

        had written so many poems   — pommes,

manzanas   — so many apples,

they all ripened on the tree   and fell down.

        Where did they land?

                         That noisy jay, busy eating

bugs, knocked them loose from where they

                      drooped,

      heavy on their boughs.

           His name is Khiḍr.

                  Federico persuaded the gardener —

        his name is Khiḍr —

to allow him to pluck a huge orange blossom

which elsewhere on the hyper-surface had gone for a walk

             up and down San Antonio

        disguised as a thirsty bitter geranium,

preferring its dirty orange fire to infinity

its poverty to the prediction of its poverty,

        which he pinned to her chiton

                        her tunic of mail.

            A moment ago

that very tunic protected Iskandar

now it is the garment of a woman so interesting, so dirty

with the filth of our time

we hardly wonder García Lorca is seized

by an impulse to adorn her neglected armor

with the flower

of

that particular tree for which Granada —

that small apple with so many seeds

that small fiery-orange bomb of love

that grenade which explodes first

inside her purplish lips

...

¿O — morena — cómo está tu cucu?

My heart beat terribly, it came

and took my breath away

        just like Sappho said.

That's a very famous line by Sappho, the line

        which asks, Oh — darkness —

                how's your cucu?

I was a student. That meant the world to me

        It was a sensible world, democratic

            stylish, inexpensive, normal

All the public time pieces had stopped

at the end of each day we never noticed

            they were always grinning

      when we looked at their faces

I had to walk for hours before I could sleep

my visits to the apple orchard became ordeals

          In my bed after midnight

there was barely room for the two of us, myself

and that pillar of mock virility which made the sheets

            a tent

...

  — when the curtain of fog touched the ground and

when, owing to its being in the time between the old

moon and the new, the shadowy darkness matched the

intellectual darkness of the age, without having betrayed

his intention to a living soul, and taking with him

nothing which might betray his identity

thereafter, he slipped away in the first hour

of curfew and disappeared without a trace

— buscando su calor

...

     buscando secretos,

        cosas perdidas

en el   olor

    muerto   del viaje

: he stood on a rocking chair, slipped

    the noose round his neck and stepped

        into the air.

Downstairs they heard the rolling   thu-tump

      thu-tump thu-tump

    of the chair   on the wooden floor

: he had grown so very thin, gaunt   sunken eyes

    which shone eagerly when he served tea

        In retrospect, he had become happy

    that soon   the bewildering   pain

    would end   In fact,   it had ended

    when he became happy   So

    why had it been necessary   to use   the noose?

    Why not go on for years   a   happy   man

    knowing that at any instant   the world

        could be disappeared?

    So little   had it come to matter

Why, it hadn't mattered at all,   the world

> nor its pain. Why,

>> that very afternoon a beautiful

young woman had come to him   delivering money

into his hand

> and the promise of more when he would go

to her room   in the hotel   next door

a woman dressed in black

>> the way the whores dress

She had decided   that morning   to share

her money   with him   for no

> other reason   than his shining

sunken   black eyes, she

> had said,   to herself,

I am going to love this man

> for all the men I do not love,   that way

my   heart

> can sing   the way it wants to,   I'm tired

of   denying

song   to my heart,   just as he is

        weary   of not

understanding why the world must be sad,   that way

his dark eyes   can shine

            as if they see hope

instead of misery, that way I can pretend

                                        to be

in union   con   las aguas

        olvidadas,   and that way

    each of us can go around the world   like

when we undress, to seek

            each other's heat.

But when she came looking for him they told her

    about the noise of the rocking chair on the wood floor

        — some melancholy tale

        of friends,

they were living on a dilapidated street in a

     poor district where last year's rubbish

        blows in the whirling wind

that street where all the loafers come and go

     where the music is loud

        defiant, indifferently ironic, vulgar

           loyalty   and betrayal

have high drama   on that street

Even the old women and men dress themselves as if

they were still lean,   sleek as the razors they held

    to each other's throats forty years ago,

and when they dance they conceal

no contempt   for imposters:

     only the ones who walk

  in a   certain

    manner,

men   and   women   who have murdered

  for love,   only those types

stay worthy   of remembrance.

: so she went back to her room   clutching the money

which had been saved to buy

                                              her heart

its   song

Not in this fucking life

One day too late

                         No one else had made tea

for her like he had,

                         the not much more

than a boy

                    with shining black eyes

...

Let the design describe

                    commensurate mind

...

La granada, entonces:

a real name

in the real fiction

Poems are not what they point at

poems are made from the names of what

they point at

names of a world

which contains the name of this world

and so very many more names

and worlds

"Only the imagination

is real!"

How can there be such a thing as a false soul?

As a black market of souls?

In this world false names

enslave the real ones

In this world why are we determined

to extirpate real names, to hunt them down

when they run away to be free amid the trees

in the forest, among the songbirds

and the elder serpents?

To imprison them, murder them, to dissect them

into properties thence recombined

to make that which is as if what had been alive alive

cool as living light but isn't

such recombinant entities aren't living names

they are such sad creatures, simulacra

bought and sold   in black markets

of false souls:

but how can a soul be false?

A false soul is not a soul?

What is it?   Where's it from?

The burst of the purples of ten thousand lips

       of laughing mouths   of women

              that   grenade

  which   a poet

          detonated   in 1920

    showers

the poem   with the blood

     of   the names

      of   the worlds

at which   that poem

    points

   his very voice   in my throat

     es decir,   en

  mi propia   garganta   está

   la sepultura de

      este poeta,   in

the throat

of the sun

      struggling

to pass   the cunning

                                                    baffles

of   the lattice,

                              al-shabaka,   designed

        to hide us from its eyes,

designed to permit entry   to the living light

            of his voice.

This world among so many whose destination

                                            whose desire

        stays us

            unknowable

                    but that we imagine it

save   that we name it

        like that apple

                    from a backyard tree

                                    like that

pomegranate   in Spain   71

        years ago

pale green   grapes

                              in a blue bowl

here in front of me,   fruits to eat, to take

              in the mouth   and eat,

they color our lips with the dye of a laughter

                              death stains

              with which death stains

                              every utterance of

                                        false names.

They are flesh   whose taste

              carries us

                    toward real destinations

                                        We change shape

        to that of a slim path

                    between extinction

                                        and the extinction

of extinction

              unknowable

              save that first we imagine

a slender path

between every idea   without exception

and its contrary,

the taste of the image

of a hyper-surface

whose pavement is light

and whose desire

is time,

or vice versa,   no importa,

a sliver   of way

sleek as the edge of a razor,

shimmering

bridge   designed

for the soul

to cross over

from its certainty

to its certainty:

Beauty

trapped in sadness

asks only to be set free,

it doesn't ask to die

nor to remain alive

in its cage.

Beauty wants to be among its own,

the ones

who love it for what it is

and for what it means.

...

One humid day in October   I saw the sight

of a boy

dancing

on the roof

of a mausoleum, over there

where that cemetery lies.

...

      Qué es buscando en inglés, ella me

pregunté.

      Looking for.

Buscando secretos   buscando mi calor

...

      She went in for gold

    gold hair

      gold slippers

a big woman   an African woman

    big enough to lift me   like a child

      gold eye-liner   gold against

su ébano   colorado, contra

    su negrura   colorada.

My how I enjoyed to look into

her   black eyes   as evenly

     as   she looked into

          my blue.

                    I made a weak fist she tied me off

eye to eye   needle like silk:

          Gold becomes you,   it flatters

                    your complexion.

Thank you she said I love gold   I said red

                              black   and gold,

some earth   of dark soils

          metals   cooked

                    in magic proportion   long ago.

Do you see red too she asked.   Of course.

     They want all of your blood

          she said Are you   in   trouble?

     "L'histoire de ma vie

          c'est le voyage et ses traces"

HEY, LA-BAS!

hey, là-bas

...

You there, thinking it over,

Chin-in-hand:

The flower of the world, brother,

did you let it pass you by?

You fool no one:

what's more useless than yesterday

if not some vain promise

of pleasure tomorrow?

...

"¿Cuándo fue?

¡NO LO SE!

...

Beauty delicate   but sufficient

    of a type like a   small black

      wrought iron fence

whose ornament doubles as a threat

         fence you see on guard

    hinges ajar, rusting   in front of old houses

in the humid   heat

    along those streets with parnassian names

      neighborhoods young greybeard strolled

some crepuscular eves

                    on Dryades   at Polymnia,   Erato

at Saint Charles,

            calliopes

tooting   in the stern   of his brain

      sailing down Euterpe,

               Religious to Race

to Wild

                    Tchoupitoulas...

     lolling on the levee

                  contemplating Algiers.

No tears.   ¿Cuándo fue?

           In the straining   dilation of

                    time's

physical   depletion,

     how many weeks ago was that?

                 Who was that

and *who* IS IT NOW

navegando   agua del

                    recuerdo,

                              whose wrinkled brow

cheered

                    by the strictest formal etiquettes, French

Spanish, even American especially Indian   Red

                         & supremely Black

     African tones,

whose dignified shoulders remember weary older oaks later on

                    walking Annunciation,

                                   having commanded all

songbirds to sing louder,

                    all oarsmen

          to pull   more rhythmically

          with still more

                                             robust joy,

                    all inspired workers

to labor   still more

          prophetically,

not for some better time,

futurity,   but for this

exquisite scented breath:

la flor del mundo

hours in New Orleans

fogging   that mirror

of man,

his duly

arrogant soul.

...

The subject is time

& the numeral,

the more of us

the less of it

save we discard

worn-out habits

of relation

"Mon sens de l'intime est vaste, n'est pas

restreint"

Our calendars don't matter, clocks

can't measure it, its instrument

which is also its measure and the organ

of its containment

"of all feelings otherwise than love

as well

as the Heart equally

holds all else there is anywhere

in Creation, when it is

<u>full</u>"

No one   nothing whatever   can possibly confine the intimacies   of our own

                    containment

                                        not months nor days

no arrivals nor leave-takings

of phenomena,   no beginnings

                    nor the aftermaths

of beginnings:

                                        what so elates the open poem

are the passersby.

...

                                        La Flor de Ebano

she goes in for ochre and red and green

she has an eager mouth,   kisses and bites

                    honey   & black pepper

        some crazy mouth it is   pussy

                        panther

teeth of coco meat

        & some milky ivory light:

her name is Sunday like some Sunday   Guillén forgot

    til he went sailing on that water,

                      that Sunday

she happened along the street.

           He watched her pass by:

silk ribbon at the nape of her neck

           smock

               made of crystal mirrors

  a girl with brand new shoulders

high heels   in a brand new way of walking:

     feverish,

       Nicolás invented

                     her new name

he called her Sugarcane

— was he unaware of the dark lords of the age,

                  cutters

who with their mochas harvest

                an ardent girl,

                        millers

who with their presses

        grind adolescence to powder?

He wasn't overlooking them he was looking at her:

                    la mulata de oro

gold-haired African, she said you have the blood of a flower,

blue-eyes,

       see it blossom in the syringe:

you better watch out when Sunday comes.

                "Nada sé, nada se sabe

                ni nada sabré jamás"

He watched her ass go by,

      talking to himself:

          the flower of the world.

                                    Bitter smoke

drifting low over the cane fields on fire.

    ...

            Now it still ripples   now it still murmurs

                        ripples

now it still   sighs

                    Smoking moon

                    aloft

                    mirrors

                    so many

                    burned-out

                    suns

have to strain

to,   must strain   harder

hungry   buscando

                    nuestros secretos

                                        buscando nuestro calor

              entre les racines nanchons

                                                In-dians

uptown rulers

              ¿Es una cosa perdida, no?

                                        No lo sé.

                                        Her brown eyes

                                        told my blue eyes

                                        blue as ice

                                        Iko Iko I   ko

              ¿Eres un caso perdido, no?

no deals

...

Tonight I heard another door close

how many of those doors are there

how many more?

Didn't you read about all those sufis weeping

for their souls in Ibn 'Arabi's

Rūḥ al-quds fī munasaḥat al-nafs?

Is it like Ulysses sobbing for his home

"some old time weird

Odysseus trip

sans paddle — up

the endless creek"?

                              May be...

who can say exactly

why some man stands weeping

at the shore of the mutable sea?

...

He sold his soul at the crossroads

                overnight

     he could play like two men

til Master Crossroads

      who's a great big powerful young thing

          Himself

set his dog

      at that young man's heels

Well, if that's how he learned, the Devil

showed him how, on a piano

        some Devil with a strong   left hand

     some Indian maybe

   someone from that nation

               yeah you're right

some bugle to wake up the nation

some furious trumpet to wake up the town

what they used to call the city

when they used to call it pretty

now it's dirty from its tuque

to its boot

                                  it only needs to shake off the dust

dusty ash from a smoking moon

fallen dusty ash

                                           from some burned-out suns

that's why spirit weeps at the crossroads

that's why lips glisten with tears

that's why she cut out su lengua

when she opens her mouth to sing she makes

the sound of water gurgling down a harsh drain

Federico asked to pin a gaudy

                    orange pomegranate flower

                         to her black tunic of mail

he brought a smile to her lips glistening with tears

sus labios   reluciendo

                                                                 con lágrimas

            les fontaines de jouvence

some old negro gardener who tends that tree

up and down San Antonio ya se va

by the name of Khiḍr

                                he plays that long slender flute

that ney of Konya

which echoes inside some tomb

        its emerald roof domed against an ice blue sky

...

It's all matter he said he would say that...

                motherfucker yo' mama

...

Tell me, brother

what time

   does that long-distance bus come down

    at the four corners

where the roads depart?

One sign laid over another sign, crossroads

    over crossroads

      eyes of fire

eyes of gold,   every which way

   to the four dark towns: Somewhere (Saviour

Nowhere (Pass

    Elsewhere (Not

      & There (By

  where the Well of

    Drumming

rises from an aquifer

billions of years below the present age

spirit moves across the waters

that ocean where the islands

                              which distribute linkage ride: they say

Spread out, little brother,

                              spread your mind abroad.

Give the wheel   (mirror mirror

on the wheel)   to Papa De Dada

Let the old man drive

                      his high window Hound

he knows well   the underwater roads

            all those

                  astronomical boulevards.

...

That's some swinging barroom door, has three atomic hinges

    full of uranium

most of these people have been here for years and years

    drinking, singing

when they are called to voice

dancing when they are called, shooting pool

   watching the fish tank, watching the

          color tv

Why, I saw a young man put his hand

       on an old lady's thigh

she didn't even move

         just laughed like she was crazy

Don't you know who I am?

No, ma'am.

    Picked up her hand

       and slapped his face

eyes like fire,

    eyes like gold, gold hair

     she wore gold slippers

she wore a dress whiter than snow in the light of the moon

she wore her hair in a black chignon

                                        tied in seven knots

or was it nine?   She flew out that door

            whizzed over the telephone wires she whizzed

over the cemetery wall   gone.

When that young man woke up they were pouring whiskey

            in his open mouth. Do you know who that was?

He couldn't talk   he was young no more.

                Son you been slapped

by the Queen.   He hasn't left this place

            from that hour til now

because that was his time. Never seen her since.

That old man you see sitting by the door, watching the fish tank

he's been old like that since he woke up

                        When you talk to him

he never says but the same few words:

the flower of the world, brother

        did you let it pass you by?

So

when the bus driver walked through that swinging

                        barroom door

the old man asked for a ticket

but that driver just laughed

        like he was crazy:

    Poor old vagabond brother,

            you've lost your way...

Want to go for a ride, old brother?

Want to spread out your sign?

              That driver, he laughed,

he walked right up to my face, eyes of fire

eyes of gold

        I stopped to take you on he said but

            I won't be stopping long:

Mirror mirror on the wheel

        now the wind's so dry and cold

        now my mind's a wall

tell my brother how I feel

                            crystal glass

time to pass

on through

to when we never knew

another   way

        to say

                          but simple words.

Don't you love the morning day

      and don't you love it after noon?   Tonight

                  twilight   air

scarcely breathes,

            evening's ordinary hearth

every relic night: in dreams

        and thoroughfares of sleep,   behold

what molten images...

themes & figures

liquified

imprints,   blows of meaning

    streaming through some medium

                not me

some personality

    who holds my life on a silver chain.

    So what if he likes to horrify

his sense of humor appeals to me

his contempt

his expert ambiguity   places everything

                in place of everything else

his customary vice, his jaw

so strong for crushing bone,   I even dig

    the diamonds   in his teeth, no one

on the street can dress so fine as that.

I've got two nickels you've got a dime,

time to spread out   de las aguas olvidadas

    des eaux là-bas.

...

One's love   is   one's undoing

        how the petal

                    fallen nearby

undoes a flower.

            See that pretty one

                        stranded over there

where the roads intersect,

                is she the only one abandoned?

She weeps so   when that last petal cuts loose

like a child   walled inside   a grown-up girl.

        Just her being here makes us fail,

            some threshold none of us can pass over,

some betrayal neither she nor we can console.

Sus lágrimas inasibles   dark   final

        Erzulie:

she speaks with such a pretty coquette's voice,   flirting

with her own inconsolable   perfection

                         how like a small child she turns her face

to the fence

                                                  to cry,

              yet she's a grown girl

all the men so handsomely perfumed,   they vie

                         for her sex

they say my caress can make her

eyes that mock them while she fucks them

                                                  they fill with tears

         to the brim,   ces fontaines

              de jouvence

                              drowning us while they watch inside

where some child   weeps   forever   alone.

                    All   the women   they   look on, they know

                                        they   don't know

all the men too

save her lovers: they are the ones   she maims for life.

...

She speaks with such a pretty coquette's voice

flirting with her own inconsolable perfection.

How the mists

of Venice   disturb

her surveillance of the moon

...

Boil it down and

boil it down

and boil it down

Samoa

...

So you can look again at Erzulie

without making a pass,

listen to her voice tell you

exactly why she is in tears.

Ask Papa Legba

Papa,

why is that girl so sad?

She's not a girl,

why do you ask me that? Don't ask me that again

or I'll take my axe

& cut your head right off

& boil it

yonder in that pit.

Don't ask.

Papa,

how come that girl weeps so?

Fool,

        she ain't no girl.

                Don't you be no fool either.

Spread out your mind.

...

                Ah, mi cucharita negra

my little black spoon,

        what are you feeding me now?

...

When lilacs last in the Captain's dooryard

      we thought we knew ourselves and what we knew

seemed itself enough   to defeat us

save there was something even more diabolical

than mutual extermination:

we became devils aswarm Africa,   common slavery

had been redundant to us, we perfected

instead exponential insult

& still we failed.

We created in America persons more than we are

inside whom we live.

All we Americans   live

contained

& sustained

inside

the moorish African race

without whom we had become extinct

and in fact are extinct

except that which of us they harbor

& to which,

wraiths of or shadows

of substantial being,

we cling all day

and night clinging not

through any conscious

relation attraction need

or affection but instead

innately   magnetized fragments   of

ephemeral   as

butterflies

psyches

cling   to vessels

which preserve us

for the hour

when this truth   bursts forth

from   ignorance

and every   triumphant

voice

shouts:

GIVE IT UP!

---

to the memory of James Carroll Booker III

Impromptu

Why would he transform familiar truth
into a toad which we must all suck?

Star jasmine flowers in his hammock
Christ, we can't make the calm permission

rain as much as clear sky, Samoa
and some more landscapes no one dares seize

don't you adore how he jams it in?
Ah, princely spirit of ale, Harry's

woofing at Jack in Will's theatred mind
track it, if only Schubert had lived

in London then, imagine Africa
extending the cable into us less the

encumbrance, bloated history
that mediocrity of time

its flag aloft in the winds
of youth, bright destiny, to the best

of our knowledge our efforts
to make it perfect recreate the world

A Tireless Magyar

Crowd of smart-looking colored women stepping
into the upstairs ballroom, as a matter of fact

I know two of them, y también esa morena, I know her:
guy would be lucky to get on the right side of

dames like them. As a matter of fact
I have been a very lucky guy

to have profited thereby:
10¢ a dance. Hello, darling,

what pleasure to see you in this light.
No, I'm not dancing tonight,

I just dropped in to hear the pianist.
You know how it is, dwindling hours

lugging around the me of my name:
I got to live up to it.

No, I don't mind at all,
it's your call.

---

to Edward Dorn

Art & Enterprise

Yeah, it was on a Hop
                              Harrigan flight to Cannibal,
Missouri when an enemy fighter intercepted
pinned us down
                              river like a bunch of tribesmen
wearing these idiotic outfits, I mean
look at us, los muñequitos

Music for Bosnian Lovers

Miles Davis was born on this day in May
heard a story about him on the radio

how he came one night where Clifford Brown
was on stage, borrowed his trumpet

to play "My Funny Valentine," finished
gave Clifford his horn back and walked out

Brownie cried, the man said
maybe it was Max Roach

but he didn't say why.
Maybe Miles's music was too much

beauty combined with too much
of its lonely disappointment.

I could have heard the story wrong, it's late
wind's rising, there's a change in the weather:

the photograph in today's newspaper is wrong
the young Serb face down in his blood, the Bosnian

girl who lived long enough to crawl
on top of him before she died too

no one can retrieve their corpses
because the son of a whore sniper

never sleeps, he's famous now
you see his smiling face in every mirror in the world.

The Noble Western Lilac At Nightfall

That's not the question the question's have you used it up?
No bodies save the passive subjective objects
that's what they want to wind up being, antenna-heads,
literally,
                    virtuals.

Deities and sympathies,
                    junk in a landfill.

Under late skies

The loop inside
the millennium, the gesture the one before had made
possible and we, we thought,
weren't —

you don't find it in your mind
it's pluvial

No Pasa Nada

Nicasio to
Tomales Bay

Petaluma to Marshall
out beyond Vallejo's baranda

his Bengali
perch

his porch
looking west

at final land
that much we have in common

mission bells
flowering in the shade

of osprey's nest.
It's a trance, isn't it?

Mire,
Umbrian shadows and all.

Poem

Who divided the earth into hemispheres?
Learned men no doubt.
My mind is divided into octaves.
Though it appear an orb of stone
set like a crude gem
into a depression
which has grown up around it,
each muscular eighth
resonates to geologic alteration.
An uplift here, there a sunken crust
every rift as pretty as a high slim waterfall.
The beach underfoot
is early sand,
millions of smooth moist rocks.
I think it's
the ingenuous honesty
of the mutables.

Listening to Frank Morgan

You shouldn't use that stuff, honey
world on a string

skin
like Italian porcelain

pink
around her nostrils

Who's In The Back Seat?

Trixie called from Walnut Creek
a girl too young among so many
strange beings half angel half sphinx
so much in love with lubricant:
Baby, you were born too late
I was born too soon
we were meant as relays
skyliners
hypnotised by phantasy, I see them all the time
kids from every corner in the world.
Debra called from West Oakland
holding a skeleton in her arms
when she opens her mouth
she's got thirty-three teeth
one's a Chiclet.

I See You

It was perfectly clear to anyone with any sense at all
that she had snapped under the burden of
memories which, after having kept dormant for
nearly twenty centuries, had come to life and waked
and were swimming through her conscious mind
and dreams like illuminated dirigibles
back and forth in a tank the size of the sky
Everyone trusts in sanity until sanity seems insane

"Yes," she said, "I was once there too, I climbed
into a tree and looked over the rooftops
until somehow I knew I had seen
the extent of the world, it was vast
and romantic, another me was somewhere out there
and it didn't matter we would never meet
it was enough, more than enough
so I climbed down from that tree and fell asleep."

She had lain there in her nap until I came along
when she started with a cry of surprise
I then saw her descending the wide stone steps
in a new brown outfit, a broad smile
and returned to my boardinghouse room
wondering who this Chinese girl could be.

---

to Aliçoun Bennett Heaton, dec. 11 Mar 93

The Rockets

Touch the dead
they teach us how to sing

        — doesn't sound like singing, does it?
Sounds like words written on a page of paper.

            The dead don't do no "sounds like."

You Can Say That

Grassland

open woodland

valleys

daytime ponds

large temporary rain pools

lakes

slowly flowing streams

creeks

brooks —

when someone says there are too many

of us

the covered bridge

explodes

into flaming pieces

they collapse

into a river so cold

and swift you'd think the

glacier's still melting.

That old bridge had been there two hundred years

offending none

yet its location acquired an unjust history

which got into the blood

of the landform

the only way that bridge had endured was denied it.

You asked for justice

                instead of satisfaction

                                of raw power

equal proportions

                equal portions

                        I see a preserve

populated sparsely

          a refuge

                an estate

but I imagine

        the pure

products anyway.

            So we are bent

by some regret,

        so what?

Nothing has begun

           to seek its own level:

go stand on the roof.

           Which ones of us,

specifically,

        are the too many?

Name one.

Cook's Hill

The bus let him off at the end of Parish Road
he walked past our house every night of the week

it was a dry town, working men
who wanted a drink had to go down to The Falls

and some women, they all had to get the last bus
up Central Ave.

He's drunk, ain't he?
No, my mother said, he's not drunk.

He doesn't drink any more, my father
said, not like he used to. Once in a while

he'll take a drink but that's all.
He walks like a drunk.

No, my father said, Charlie used to be an alky
but he walks like that because he was burnt.

You can't see it, my mother said, unless you get close
to his hands, but his legs

and part of his body are burned. He
can't help but walk that way.

He fell asleep smoking, my father said, the mattress
caught fire. Murray saved his life.

Saved the house too.
That's what makes him limp so.

He's a nice man, my mother said. He was always
a nice man, even when he was drinking.

They both are, those two,
they don't bother anybody.

Don't Get Me Wrong

Some tiny island
every day it rains

colored people live there
people like me

when we were kids
we ran in the ruts of the road

the known world
always

Why Ain't You Married?

I am married.

Where's your husband?

Right over there.

Where? I don't see nothing

        except that goat.

That's him alright.

So they cut that creature's throat

        they cut off his organ of creation

and they cut off the hand with

        which he wrote.

What's his name?

He is called Hand to Hand.

---

homage to Zora Neale Hurston

Prosthetics

I went to see the fortune teller, Madame Laveau.
"I see an ophiolithic rendezvous

                            for you, my man, an upthrust
of warm hips and backsides.
Quite the huevón, aren't you?"
Well, I said, I do my darnedest.
"Do better than that, will you, honey,

                 Pisces is just about drained."
What can you recommend, Madame Marie?
"Foxing the goose. Definitely. Most guys who consult me
I advise them, goose the fox, but you, sir,
if you can get your mitts on a willing artifice,
maybe you'll profit from a suck on her copper tits."
You can't mean that! I protested. "I do," she said,
"the softer the pillow lava the sweeter the hive."

Cotton Tail

Whatcha gonna do when the mirror turns on you?
You gonna talk to it?

        Or are you going to listen to it?

"I am your reflection,

        I am not you —

                not yet I'm not,
but it's in the works."

I hear a lot of guys like the river bank,

        maybe I would too,

             strolling along with the girls
who work for a living,
I hear their afternoons are free:

do you know what it means to miss me?

Sicily Island

Sonny, we hated to see
        you go
but a man cannot live in the world of the obvious

Nothing like a slow old train on a bright July day
        riding up top alongside some pretty tune playing
inside the mind

...thinking about the other girls
        on the street they hope to meet
a gentle funny young man who can take care of himself

        a lot to ask
but then a lot to give.
I met someone like that
        I don't even remember what we talked about
you don't know how many loves
        shattered the time barrier
you forget their names.

        I tried to make you happy
        in the time we had
but I could see you slipping away
        down to the yards,
        qué pena —
what to make of innocence.

It rolls across the land

on pretty white wheels

made of what my mind's made of
now that it's on you.

Darling, I don't know how
many more nights like this one
I can take

— some morning soon
it all has to live up to itself.

No Meaning For Him

His nostalgic memory
                    owed to art
                              its reach —
women coming and going
                    noisily shutting doors
come Napoletane
                    old ones, young
plenty to grab on to
                    plenty more to hold tight
Always the search for the ideal city
where the south
                    and the north
                              perfectly mix:

women independent of
                    all
                              save their flesh.

Torcher

Come to mama, my man —

                  squeeze my hand

til Jesse James

               I'm sure you're familiar with that

Poem

Yeah, I stole from
                         the treasury
of human folly
I spent it all on you, baby...

don't mention it

Poem

What it is that makes sleep so hard in the secret world?
Caged in

        muros de pintura inasible

                dusty summertime shoes

standing by.

View in threes and fours

Bright moon,

            warm wind —

Shao's lights.

Hours ago, stripped to the waist

        in an arbor

                of nasturtiums

brushing his teeth.

1993